AI BASICS &

THE RGB PROMPT

ENGINEERING MODEL

Empowering AI Through Effective

Prompt Engineering

A Guide for AI, ChatGPT & Google Bard Enthusiasts

PHILL AKINWALE, OPM3, PMP

AI Basics & The RGB Prompt Engineering Model
Published by Praizion Media
P.O Box 22241, Mesa, AZ 85277
E-mail: info@praizion.com
www.praizion.com

Author
Phillip Akinwale, MSc, OPM3, PMP, PMI-ACP, CAPM, PSM, CSM

ISBN 978-1-934579-22-0

9 781934 579220

CONTENTS

CHAPTER 1
INTRODUCTION

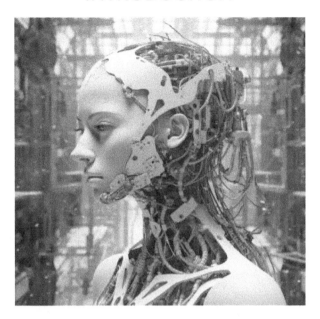

In the year 2023, the world witnessed a monumental shift in the way we interacted with technology. Artificial Intelligence (AI) took center stage, captivating the imaginations of people from all walks of life. But what is AI? Let's get that question answered!

What is Artificial Intelligence (AI)?

Artificial Intelligence (AI) refers to the simulation of human intelligence processes by machines, especially computer systems. These processes include learning (the acquisition of information and rules for using the information), reasoning (using the rules to reach approximate or definite conclusions), and self-correction.

AI is an interdisciplinary science with multiple approaches, but advancements in machine learning and deep learning are creating a paradigm shift in virtually every sector of the tech industry. Machine learning is a method of data analysis that automates analytical model building. It's a branch of artificial intelligence based on the idea that systems can learn from data, identify patterns, and make decisions with minimal human intervention. Deep learning, a subset of machine learning, utilizes a hierarchical level of artificial neural networks to carry out the process of machine learning. The artificial neural networks are built like the human brain, with neuron nodes connected together like a web.

AI applications can be grouped into two types: narrow AI, which is designed to perform a narrow task such as voice recognition, and general AI, which is AI that can understand, learn, and apply knowledge in a broad range of tasks at a level equal to or beyond a human being. For a long time until only very recently, general AI remains largely in the realm of science fiction, with no systems displaying such comprehensive ability.

In summary, AI involves creating algorithms that allow computers to mimic human behavior, it's used in a vast array of applications, from voice assistants like Alexa or Siri to recommendation engines like those of Netflix or Amazon, to autonomous vehicles, medical diagnosis, and many more.

Among the many AI breakthroughs, one technology stood out as a game-changer – ChatGPT. Developed by OpenAI, ChatGPT became a sensation, captivating users with its ability to generate human-like text and engage in dynamic conversations. The AI community and enthusiasts alike were left in awe of its capabilities.

As the AI landscape rapidly evolved, there emerged a strong demand for knowledge and understanding of ChatGPT and its underlying principles. People craved to unravel the secrets behind this groundbreaking technology and harness its power for their own purposes. Recognizing this growing need, I decided to embark on a journey to demystify the intricacies of ChatGPT and explore the fascinating world of prompt engineering.

Within a few days of announcing my ChatGPT and AI course, an influx of eager students signed up, hungry for knowledge and determined to stay ahead of the curve. It became evident that there was an insatiable thirst for understanding the inner workings of ChatGPT and the art of prompt engineering. Students from diverse backgrounds, including professionals, researchers, and enthusiasts, recognized the transformative potential of AI and sought to master this cutting-edge technology.

This book, " The RGB Prompt Engineering Model: Empowering AI Through Effective Prompt Engineering," serves as a comprehensive resource to meet this demand and provide invaluable insights into the world of AI. It delves deep into the intricacies of ChatGPT, exploring its capabilities, limitations, and the underlying mechanisms that make it function.

The relevance of this book lies in its ability to equip readers with the knowledge and skills to leverage the power of ChatGPT and prompt engineering. Whether you are a professional seeking to enhance your AI capabilities, a researcher delving into the frontiers of AI technology, or an enthusiast eager to explore the possibilities of ChatGPT, this book caters to your needs.

AI has come a long way! The table that follows provides a chronological overview of the key milestones in the development of Artificial Intelligence (AI), from ancient times to the present. It details the conceptual foundations, significant events, key people, and organizations that have shaped the evolution of this groundbreaking technology. Beginning with the ancient vision of artificial beings and moving through philosophical, mechanical, and technological developments, this table charts the journey of AI over the centuries. It illustrates the ebbs and flows of interest and innovation in the field, culminating in the present era, where AI is a transformative force across many industries.

AI Timeline of Major Milestones

Date	Development/Milestone	Key People/Firm
Antiquity	The idea of creating artificial beings is envisioned	Ancient Greece and Egypt societies
17th century	Proposal that the mind could be explained in terms of mechanics	René Descartes, Gottfried Leibniz
1800s	Creation of the first industrial software: a programmable loom	Joseph Marie Jacquard
1822–1859	Work on programmable mechanical calculating machines	Charles Babbage, Ada Lovelace
1900s	Publication of Principia Mathematica, revolutionizing formal logic	Bertrand Russell, Alfred North Whitehead
1930s	Discovery of limits to what machines can do	Kurt Gödel, Alonzo Church
1940s	Publication of work on the Turing machine, foundation of modern computer science	Alan Turing
1950s	Coined "artificial intelligence", held the Dartmouth AI Summer Research Project	John McCarthy
1960s	First AI programs were developed, including the chatbot ELIZA	Various researchers
1970s	AI field experienced a period of decline	Various factors
1980s	Recovery of AI field with the development of new techniques	Various researchers
1990s	Rapid growth in AI field due to new technologies	Various researchers
2000s	Growth of AI field with machine learning and deep learning techniques	Various researchers
2010	Launch of Kinect for Xbox 360, tracking human body movement	Microsoft
2011	Organization of the First AAAI Workshop on AI and Sustainability	Mary Lou Maher, Doug Fisher
2011–2014	Smartphone apps Siri, Google Now and Cortana	Apple, Google, Microsoft
2016	Google DeepMind's AlphaGo defeated Lee Sedol in Go	Google DeepMind
2017	Asilomar Conference on Beneficial AI, Discussion on AI ethics and Deepstack defeating human players in poker	Various researchers, Deepstack
2017	AlphaGo Zero learned by playing only against itself and displayed significant performance gains	Google DeepMind
2018	Alibaba language processing AI outperforms top humans at a reading and comprehension test	Alibaba
2019	DeepMind's AlphaStar reaches Grandmaster level at StarCraft II	Google DeepMind
2020	Introduction of Turing Natural Language Generation (T-NLG) and OpenAI's GPT-3	Microsoft, OpenAI
2022	Launch of ChatGPT	OpenAI
2023	Release of GPT-4 and Google Bard	OpenAI, Google

The journey forward

Through the lens of real-world applications and practical examples, this book aims to demystify the complexities of prompt engineering. Prompt engineering serves as the backbone of ChatGPT, allowing users to input precise instructions and generate tailored responses. By understanding the Role - Goal - Benefit (RGB) model, readers will learn how to craft prompts that extract the desired outputs from ChatGPT.

The journey within these pages will take you through the fundamentals of AI and prompt engineering, exploring topics such as the importance of clear task definition, identification of key inputs and outputs, the art of natural language prompts, and the significance of context in prompt engineering. Additionally, you will discover the power of incorporating domain-specific knowledge and active verbs to create prompts that deliver precise and relevant results.

This book goes beyond theory and immerses readers in practical applications. From generating compelling arguments to designing tabular views and creating product backlogs, you will witness the power of prompt engineering in action. Through real-world scenarios and examples, you will gain the necessary skills to effectively harness ChatGPT and prompt engineering to drive success in your endeavors.

In conclusion, " The RGB Prompt Engineering Model: Empowering AI Through Effective Prompt Engineering" is your gateway to mastering the transformative world of AI. This book stands as a testament to the tremendous demand for knowledge and understanding in this rapidly evolving field. Whether you are a seasoned professional or an aspiring enthusiast, the insights, techniques, and practical applications outlined in this book will empower you to unlock the full potential of ChatGPT and prompt engineering, and navigate the AI revolution with confidence. Let us embark on this enlightening journey together

CHAPTER 1: INTRODUCTION EXERCISE

1. Write a short essay describing your understanding of AI before starting this book.
2. Discuss the various ways AI has already impacted your daily life.
3. Research one AI pioneer mentioned in the AI timeline of major milestones and prepare a short presentation on their contributions.

CHAPTER 2
INTRODUCTION TO AI

This course in a book will provide an overview of the field of artificial intelligence, including its history, key concepts, and applications. Students will learn about the different types of AI, such as machine learning, natural language processing, and computer vision. They will also learn about the ethical considerations involved in AI development and lastly prompt engineering which will cover a huge part of this book.

I. Definition of Artificial Intelligence:

Artificial Intelligence (AI) is a branch of computer science that focuses on creating machines or software with the ability to exhibit intelligence comparable to human intelligence. It encompasses the development of systems that can learn from experience, adapt to new inputs, comprehend complex concepts, and perform tasks that typically require human intelligence.

II. History of Artificial Intelligence:

The history of Artificial Intelligence traces its roots from its philosophical origins to its practical implementation. It began as a field of study and speculation in the 1950s, with early pioneers like Alan Turing and John McCarthy. The initial years witnessed the development of symbolic AI, where researchers focused on programming rules and logic to mimic human intelligence. The era of expert systems followed, which involved the creation of specialized systems capable of solving specific problems. In recent years, machine learning and deep learning have gained prominence, allowing AI systems to learn and make decisions based on vast amounts of data.

III. Key Concepts of AI:

1. **Machine Learning (ML):** Machine Learning is a subset of AI that concentrates on designing systems capable of learning from data and making decisions. It can be categorized into various types:

   - Supervised Learning: In this approach, algorithms learn patterns from labeled data to make predictions or classify new instances.

   - Unsupervised Learning: Here, algorithms learn patterns and structures from unlabeled data without specific guidance.

   - Semi-supervised Learning: This method combines both labeled and unlabeled data to train models.

   - Reinforcement Learning: It involves training models to make decisions based on trial-and-error interactions with an environment, receiving feedback in the form of rewards or penalties.

2. **Natural Language Processing (NLP):** NLP deals with the interaction between computers and human language. It enables computers to understand, interpret, and generate human language in a meaningful way. Key concepts in NLP include:

- Syntax: The study of the grammatical rules and structure of language.
- Semantics: The interpretation of meaning in language and the understanding of context.
- Discourse: The analysis of language beyond individual sentences, focusing on coherence and cohesion.
- Speech: The processing and understanding of spoken language.

3. **Computer Vision:** Computer Vision aims to equip machines with the ability to visually perceive and comprehend the world. It encompasses various concepts such as:

- Image Recognition: Identifying and classifying objects or patterns within images.
- Object Detection: Locating and recognizing specific objects within an image or video.
- Image Segmentation: Dividing an image into meaningful segments to extract information.
- Scene Reconstruction: Creating 3D representations of scenes or objects from 2D images or videos.

4. **Artificial Neural Networks (ANNs):** Artificial Neural Networks are computational systems inspired by the structure and functioning of biological neural networks found in animal brains. They play a fundamental role in advanced AI models such as deep learning. ANNs consist of interconnected artificial neurons that process and transmit information.

Artificial neural networks (ANNs) are a type of machine learning algorithm that are inspired by the human brain. They are made up of interconnected nodes, which are similar to neurons in the brain. ANNs can be used to solve a variety of problems, including classification, regression, and forecasting.

In project management, ANNs can be used to:

- Identify risks: ANNs can be used to analyze historical data to identify patterns that may indicate potential risks for future projects.
- Estimate costs: ANNs can be used to analyze historical data to estimate the cost of future projects.
- Schedule projects: ANNs can be used to analyze historical data to schedule future projects.

- Manage resources: ANNs can be used to analyze historical data to manage resources for future projects.
- Communicate with stakeholders: ANNs can be used to generate reports and visualizations that can be used to communicate with stakeholders about project status and risks.

ANNs are a powerful tool that can be used to improve project management. However, it is important to note that ANNs are not a silver bullet. They are only as good as the data they are trained on. If the data is not accurate or complete, the ANN will not be able to produce accurate results.

Here are some of the benefits of using ANNs in project management:

- Improved accuracy: ANNs can be used to improve the accuracy of predictions and estimates.
- Increased efficiency: ANNs can be used to automate tasks, which can free up project managers to focus on more strategic and creative work.

- Reduced risk: ANNs can be used to identify and mitigate risks, which can help to improve project success rates.

Here are some of the challenges of using ANNs in project management:

- Data requirements: ANNs require large amounts of data to train. This data can be difficult and expensive to acquire.
- Model complexity: ANNs can be complex models, which can make them difficult to understand and interpret.
- Overfitting: ANNs can be prone to overfitting, which occurs when the model learns the training data too well and is unable to generalize to new data.
- Overall, ANNs are a powerful tool that can be used to improve project management.

5. **Deep Learning:** Deep Learning is a subset of machine learning that utilizes artificial neural networks, particularly deep neural networks, to learn from vast amounts of data. These networks have multiple hidden layers, allowing them to automatically extract

hierarchical representations of data, leading to advanced pattern recognition and decision-making capabilities.

IV. Applications of AI:

AI finds applications in various fields, revolutionizing industries and enhancing numerous processes. Some key applications include:

1. Predictive Analytics: AI algorithms can analyze historical data to identify patterns, trends, and make predictions about future outcomes, aiding decision-making in areas like finance, marketing, and weather forecasting.

2. Automated Transportation: AI is driving the development of autonomous vehicles, optimizing traffic management systems, and enhancing transportation safety.

3. Virtual Personal Assistants: AI-powered virtual assistants like Siri, Alexa, and Google Assistant provide personalized assistance to users, performing tasks such as setting reminders, answering questions, and controlling smart devices.

4. Content Delivery: AI algorithms analyze user preferences and behavior to deliver personalized content recommendations, enhancing user experience

in areas like streaming services, news platforms, and e-commerce.

5. Fraud Detection: AI systems can detect patterns and anomalies in large volumes of data, helping to identify fraudulent activities and protect against financial fraud and cybersecurity threats.

6. Precision Medicine: AI is utilized in healthcare to analyze medical data, genetics, and patient records, enabling personalized treatment plans, drug discovery, and medical diagnosis.

V. Ethical Considerations in AI Development:

As AI continues to advance, there are important ethical considerations that need to be addressed. Key considerations include:

1. Bias and Fairness: AI algorithms can unintentionally reflect biases present in training data, leading to unfair or discriminatory outcomes. Ensuring fairness and mitigating bias is crucial in AI development.

2. Transparency and Explainability: AI systems often operate as black boxes, making it difficult to understand the reasoning behind their decisions. There is a need for transparency and explainability to build trust and accountability.

3. Privacy and Security: AI systems process and analyze vast amounts of personal data, raising concerns about privacy and data security. Safeguarding data and ensuring user privacy is essential.

4. Job Automation and Economic Implications: AI's impact on the workforce and job automation is a significant consideration. It is important to understand and address the potential economic implications of AI-driven automation.

5. Regulation and Policy: The development and deployment of AI technologies require appropriate regulations and policies to address ethical concerns, protect users, and ensure responsible use.

VI. Future of AI:

The future of AI holds immense potential for advancements and applications. Some areas of exploration include:

1. Advanced Robotics: AI-powered robots with enhanced perception, dexterity, and decision-making capabilities are expected to play significant roles in industries such as manufacturing, healthcare, and exploration.

2. Explainable AI: Efforts are being made to develop AI systems that can provide transparent explanations for their decisions, enhancing trust and understanding.

3. AI in Augmented Reality (AR) and Virtual Reality (VR): The integration of AI with AR and VR technologies can create immersive and intelligent virtual environments, impacting fields like gaming, training simulations, and virtual communication.

4. AI in Climate Change and Sustainability: AI can contribute to addressing climate change challenges by optimizing energy systems, improving resource management, and enabling more sustainable practices.

CHAPTER 2: INTRODUCTION TO AI EXERCISE

1. Discuss the ethical considerations of developing and deploying AI technologies.

2. Get AI to Write a simple HTML, JavaScript or Python program to implement a simple AI that can play a game like Space-invaders, Tic-Tac-Toe, a simple quiz or Checkers.

CHAPTER 3
FUNDAMENTALS OF MACHINE LEARNING

We will start by introducing the fundamental concepts and principles of machine learning. Machine learning (ML) is a subset of artificial intelligence that involves the use of algorithms and statistical models to perform tasks without explicit programming. Core principles include concepts such as training and testing data, overfitting and underfitting, bias-variance tradeoff, and the general process of model selection and evaluation.

Supervised Learning:

In supervised learning, we have a set of labeled training data. Each instance in the training set contains the input features and the corresponding correct output, or 'label'. The goal of supervised learning is to train a model that, given the input features, can accurately predict the output. This can be used for classification problems (where the output is a category, like spam or not-spam) or regression problems (where the output is a continuous value, like house price).

Unsupervised Learning:

Unsupervised learning involves training on data that has not been labeled. The machine learning algorithm tries to learn the underlying structure of the data, or to summarize it in some way. This can include clustering (grouping similar instances together), anomaly detection (finding unusual instances), and dimensionality reduction (simplifying the data without losing too much information).

Reinforcement Learning:

In reinforcement learning, an agent learns how to behave in an environment by performing actions and getting rewards or penalties in return. The goal is to develop a policy, which is a strategy that defines what action the agent should take under certain circumstances. Reinforcement learning is particularly useful for problems where there is a sequence of decisions to be made (like a game of chess).

Reinforcement Learning Algorithms

- Markov decision processes (MDPs) are a mathematical framework for modeling decision-making problems in an uncertain environment. An MDP is defined by a set of states, a set of actions, a transition function, a reward function, and a discount factor. The state of an MDP represents the current situation of the agent. The actions available to the agent are the things that the agent can do to change its state. The transition function describes how the state of the MDP changes when the agent takes an action. The reward function describes how much reward the agent receives when it enters a particular state. The discount factor determines how much weight is given to future rewards.

- Q-learning is a reinforcement learning algorithm that learns to map states to actions that maximize expected reward. Q-learning works by iteratively updating a table that stores the expected reward for taking each action in each state. The table is updated using the Bellman equation, which is a recursive equation that describes the relationship between the expected reward for taking an action in a state and the expected reward for taking an action in a subsequent state.

- Policy gradients is a reinforcement learning algorithm that learns to map states to probabilities of taking actions. Policy gradients work by iteratively updating a policy function that maps states to probabilities of taking actions. The policy function is updated using the policy gradient theorem, which is a theorem that describes how the expected reward for a policy can be improved by changing the policy function.

Different Machine Learning Algorithms:

This refers to exploring a variety of algorithms used in machine learning, beyond the broad categories of supervised, unsupervised, and reinforcement learning. This could include specific algorithms like decision trees, neural networks, support vector machines, etc. Each algorithm has its strengths and weaknesses and is suitable for different types of tasks.

Application of Machine Learning to Real-World Problems:

Machine learning can be used to solve a wide range of real-world problems. This could include anything from predicting stock prices, recommending products to customers, detecting fraudulent transactions, to driving autonomous vehicles. The key is to identify a problem where machine learning can be effectively applied, to prepare the data correctly, to choose the right algorithm, and to tune it for optimal performance.

CHAPTER 3: FUNDAMENTALS OF MACHINE LEARNING EXERCISE

1. Explain the difference between supervised and unsupervised learning.

2. Discuss the importance of data in machine learning.

3. Visit the website for a machine learning library like Scikit-learn and browse the content.

CHAPTER 4
FUNDAMENTALS OF NATURAL LANGUAGE
PROCESSING

Natural Language Processing (NLP) is a subfield of artificial intelligence that focuses on the interaction between computers and humans through natural language. The ultimate objective of NLP is to read, decipher, understand, and make sense of human language in a valuable way. Key concepts include tokenization (breaking text into words, phrases, or other meaningful elements), part-of-speech tagging, syntax tree parsing, and semantic analysis (understanding meaning from the text).

Text Classification:

Text classification is a type of supervised learning that assigns predefined categories (or labels) to text. It's used in several applications, such as email spam detection, document categorization, sentiment analysis, and more. It involves learning from a training set of labeled documents and then using the learned model to classify new documents. Algorithms used for text classification can include Naive Bayes, Support Vector Machines (SVM), and deep learning models like Convolutional Neural Networks (CNN) or Recurrent Neural Networks (RNN).

Sentiment Analysis:

Sentiment analysis, also referred to as opinion mining, uses NLP, text analysis, and computational linguistics to identify and extract subjective information from source materials. It's about determining the attitude, sentiments, evaluations, appraisals, and emotions of a speaker/writer based on the computational treatment of subjectivity in a text. This can be particularly useful for social media monitoring, brand monitoring, and understanding customer feedback.

Question Answering:

Question answering (QA) is a computer science discipline within the fields of information retrieval and natural language processing (NLP), which is concerned with building systems that automatically answer questions posed by humans in a natural language. This involves understanding the question, finding the relevant data, and delivering the answer in a human-understandable form. QA systems can be rule-based, where a set of pre-determined rules guide the system to generate an answer, or they can be machine learning-based, where the system is trained on a large dataset of question-answer pairs.

How to Apply Natural Language Processing to Real-World Problems:

Applying NLP to real-world problems involves understanding the problem context, selecting the right NLP techniques, preprocessing the data properly, and effectively implementing the chosen models. Some common real-world applications of NLP include:

- **Information Extraction:** Extracting structured information from unstructured text data. For example, identifying the key entities mentioned in news articles.

- **Text Summarization:** Automatically generating a concise summary of a long text. This is useful for quickly understanding the content of a document without reading the whole thing.

- **Machine Translation:** Translating text from one language to another. This is the technology behind services like Google Translate.

- **Chatbots and Virtual Assistants:** These applications understand natural language instructions and respond in kind, enabling humans to interact with software in a natural, conversational way.

CHAPTER 4: FUNDAMENTALS OF NATURAL LANGUAGE PROCESSING EXERCISE

1. Use ChatGPT to Research and explain the role of tokenization in Natural Language Processing (NLP).

2. Discuss the challenges of understanding context in NLP.

CHAPTER 5
FUNDAMENTALS OF COMPUTER VISION

Computer vision is a field of artificial intelligence that trains computers to interpret and understand the visual world. In other words, with computer vision, machines can visually sense the world, and interpret its content just like humans do. This involves processes like acquiring, processing, analyzing, and understanding digital images, and extraction of high-dimensional data from the real world in order to produce numerical or symbolic information. The fundamental concepts in computer vision include image processing techniques, feature extraction, and 3D reconstruction.

Object Detection:

Object detection is a computer vision technique for locating instances of objects in images or videos. It's a key technology behind applications like video surveillance, image retrieval systems, and autonomous vehicles, where it's crucial to understand the context of what's being seen in an image. Object detection models are usually trained using supervised learning algorithms. They combine the use of object localization (to locate the presence of an object in an image and indicate it with a bounding box) and object classification (to predict the type of object that was localized).

Image Classification:

Image classification is the process of categorizing and labeling groups of pixels or vectors within an image based on specific rules. The task of image classification is to take an input image and predict the class of the image. This is a type of supervised learning where the model is trained with a dataset of input images and their respective classes. Once trained, the model can classify new input images into these classes. Convolutional Neural Networks (CNNs) are commonly used for image classification tasks due to their success in capturing spatial information in an image.

Face Recognition:

Face recognition is a method of identifying or verifying the identity of an individual using their face. This involves several steps: face detection (finding faces in images), face alignment (aligning faces based on eye positions or other landmarks), feature extraction (extracting features from the aligned face that can be used to represent the face), and finally face matching or classification (comparing the features to a database of known faces). The feature extraction step is often done with a deep learning model, where a Convolutional Neural Network (CNN) is trained to output a compact but rich representation of the face.

Computer vision techniques are used across various domains like medical imaging, self-driving cars, image restoration, and more. Learning these topics will provide a good foundation for anyone looking to dive deeper into the field of computer vision.

CHAPTER 5: FUNDAMENTALS OF COMPUTER VISION

1. Explain how convolutional neural networks are used in computer vision.
2. Discuss the applications and limitations of computer vision.

CHAPTER 6
FUNDAMENTALS OF PROMPT ENGINEERING

In this chapter, we will explore the fascinating topic of prompt engineering and its significance in the field of artificial intelligence. Prompt engineering plays a crucial role in ensuring that AI models produce precise and robust outputs based on the given prompts.

A Case for Prompt Engineering

As AI continues to advance and integrate into various aspects of our lives, it becomes essential to understand how prompts shape the behavior and decision-making of AI models. The prompts we provide act as instructions that guide the AI in generating the desired outputs. Therefore, the quality and specificity of the prompts directly impact the accuracy and relevance of the AI's responses.

Prompt engineering is particularly crucial in the realm of natural language processing (NLP), where AI models are designed to understand and generate human-like language. By carefully designing prompts, we can ensure that the AI accurately comprehends the task at hand and generates responses that meet our expectations.

The importance of precise and robust prompts cannot be overstated. They serve as the foundation for effective communication with AI models, enabling us to extract the desired information or achieve specific tasks. When prompts are vague or poorly constructed, the AI may struggle to understand our intentions, resulting in inaccurate or irrelevant outputs.

Good vs. Bad Prompts

Consider a scenario where we want to translate a sentence to French. A poor prompt would be "Translate this sentence to French," as it lacks the necessary information. In contrast, a good prompt would be "Please translate the following sentence into French: 'I would like to order a coffee and a croissant.'" The latter prompt provides clear instructions and specific details, ensuring that the AI understands our request accurately.

Another example can be seen in a writing task. Asking the AI to "Write a short story" is vague and leaves room for interpretation. However, a more effective prompt would be "Write a 500-word short story that includes the following three elements: a red balloon, a deserted beach, and a mysterious stranger." By providing specific criteria, we guide the AI's creativity and ensure that the resulting story aligns with our intentions.

Explicit Prompts

Explicit prompts are commands or instructions that precisely articulate the task the model needs to perform. These prompts are characterized by clarity and specificity. They leave little to no room for ambiguity, as they detail the nature of the output the user expects.

An explicit prompt can be as simple as "Write a poem about a flower." Here, the user is expressly asking the language model to compose a poem, and the subject of the poem is clearly defined as a flower. The instruction is direct and unambiguous.

Explicit prompts can also be more complex, requiring the model to perform tasks involving a series of steps. For example, consider the explicit prompt, "Read the following text and summarize it in three sentences." The model is clearly instructed first to read or process a given text and then to produce a summary condensed into three sentences.

The effectiveness of explicit prompts lies in their precision. They provide a roadmap that the model can follow, enabling it to generate responses that align closely with the user's intent.

Explicit prompts also enhance the model's ability to handle tasks that require a structured response. In the context of a writing task, for instance, an explicit prompt like "Write an essay discussing the causes and effects of climate change" will guide the model to produce an essay that not only addresses the specific topic (climate change) but also covers the specific aspects of the topic (causes and effects).

Explicit prompts can be particularly useful in educational and professional applications. They can guide language models to generate specific and structured responses or content, such as essays, reports, lesson plans, business plans, code snippets, and more.

Implicit Prompts

Implicit prompts, on the other hand, convey the task to the language model in a less direct manner. These prompts are often more open-ended, leaving room for interpretation. The user is still guiding the model's response but in a less restrictive way, allowing the model to generate a broader range of responses.

Take the implicit prompt "Describe a flower," for example. This instruction doesn't specify the format or structure of the response. The model could choose to describe a flower scientifically, focusing on its biological characteristics. Alternatively, it could take a more poetic approach, describing the flower's beauty and fragrance. The prompt guides the model to provide information about a flower, but the nature and style of the response are left open-ended.

Implicit prompts stimulate the model to exhibit its creative and generative capabilities. For instance, if a user provides the prompt, "It was a dark and stormy night," the model might generate a suspenseful short story, an atmospheric poem, or a descriptive paragraph. The ambiguity allows for a multitude of possible responses, each displaying the model's ability to create original content based on the given trigger.

Implicit prompts also allow users to explore the model's ability to adapt to context and extrapolate from incomplete information. For example, if a user provides the prompt, "As the sun set," the model could continue the narrative in a variety of ways, depending on the context provided or inferred.

Implicit prompts can prove useful in a range of scenarios, particularly those that benefit from creativity, variety, and exploration. They can help generate diverse narrative content, ideate for brainstorming sessions, or even assist in creating various forms of artistic expression, such as stories, poems, and scripts.

Prompts in Image Generation

In the same vein, prompt engineering plays a crucial role in image generation tasks. When requesting an image from an AI, it is essential to provide clear and precise prompts regarding the desired style, subject matter, and other visual characteristics. For example, instead of simply asking the AI to "Generate an image of a cat," a better prompt would be "Please generate an image of a white Persian cat sitting on a windowsill, looking out at the moonlit city skyline." This level of detail ensures that the AI produces an image that matches our specific requirements.

Good Prompt Structure

Prompt engineering involves designing prompts that are concise, focused, and accurately convey the intended meaning. It requires careful consideration of the context in which the prompts will be used and tailoring them accordingly. For instance, a prompt designed for a chatbot would differ from one designed for language translation.

Active verbs can bring more energy and urgency to prompts, making them more effective in guiding the AI's decision-making. Additionally, incorporating relevant domain-specific knowledge into prompts helps align the AI's responses with the desired outcomes. It is also crucial to consider the audience for whom the prompts are intended, as this influences the language and tone used in the prompts.

To ensure the effectiveness of prompts, it is essential to test them with real users and gather feedback on their clarity and effectiveness. Continuous iteration and improvement of prompt design based on user feedback and performance metrics lead to more effective AI models.

The Importance of Good Prompts

Prompt engineering is a critical aspect of developing AI models that can generate high-quality outputs meeting the needs and expectations of users. By mastering the art of prompt engineering, we can leverage the power of AI to automate tasks, enhance decision-making processes, and streamline various aspects of our lives.

3 Rules for Effective Prompts

1. Be clear and concise. The Large Language Model (LLM) should be able to understand what you are asking for without having to guess.
2. Provide enough context. The more context you provide, the better the LLM will be able to generate a response.
3. Be specific. The more specific you are, the more likely the LLM is to generate a response that is relevant to your needs.

Why the RGB Model?

In the following chapters, we will dive deeper into the intricacies of prompt engineering, exploring various techniques and examples to illustrate its practical application. We will examine the Role-Goal-Benefit (RGB) prompt language model, which is derived from the concept of user stories and offers a structured approach to prompt design.

The RGB model allows us to define roles, goals, and benefits within our prompts, providing a clear framework for the AI to understand the context and purpose of the task. By crafting prompts using this model, we can enhance the precision and effectiveness of our interactions with AI models.

Imagine you are a sales representative for a software company. Your goal is to sell a new project management software to a potential customer, with the benefit of increased productivity. Using the RGB model, you would frame your prompt as follows: "As a sales representative for a software company, your goal is to sell our new project management software to a potential customer. By doing so, you will help increase their productivity and streamline their project management processes, leading to more efficient and effective project delivery."

By structuring the prompt in this manner, you provide the AI with a clear understanding of your role, the desired outcome, and the benefits associated with achieving that outcome. This level of specificity helps the AI generate responses that align with your intentions and objectives.

Various Industries

Prompt engineering is not limited to sales or business-related scenarios. It is equally applicable in educational settings. Suppose you are a primary school teacher introducing a new interactive learning tool to your students, aiming to increase student engagement and improve learning outcomes. Using the RGB model, you can frame your prompt as follows: "As a primary school teacher, your goal is to introduce a new interactive learning tool to your students. By doing so, you will increase student engagement and create an environment conducive to improved learning outcomes. Incorporating this tool into the classroom will enhance student participation and motivation, leading to improved academic performance."

Again, the prompt sets a clear context for the AI, allowing it to generate responses that address the specific objectives and benefits associated with introducing the learning tool.

Prompt engineering also plays a crucial role in marketing. Suppose you are a marketing manager for a retail brand tasked with launching a new clothing line for the upcoming season, aiming to increase sales and brand awareness. Using the RGB model, you can structure your prompt as follows: "As a marketing manager for a retail brand, your goal is to launch our new clothing line for the upcoming season. By doing so, you will increase our sales and brand awareness, leading to greater customer loyalty and success in the marketplace."

By providing this prompt, you enable the AI to understand the marketing objectives and align its responses with the desired outcomes. This level of precision and clarity allows for more effective collaboration between human and AI.

Project managers, too, can leverage the power of prompt engineering in their work. Suppose you are a project manager for a construction firm with the goal of completing a new building project on time and within budget, aiming to satisfy clients and increase the company's reputation in the industry. Using the RGB model, you can frame your prompt as follows: "As a project manager for a construction firm, your goal is to complete our new building project on time and within budget. By doing so, you will satisfy our clients and increase our reputation in the industry, leading to more business opportunities and continued success."'

The precision and focus of this prompt empower the AI to understand the project manager's role and objectives, guiding its responses to align with the desired outcomes.

Throughout the following chapters, we will delve deeper into the practical application of prompt engineering, providing more examples and techniques for crafting effective prompts. We will explore different types of prompts, such as direct prompts and prompts by example, and discuss the importance of using active verbs, incorporating domain-specific knowledge, and considering the context in which prompts will be used.

Prompt engineering is a critical aspect of developing effective AI models that can generate high-quality outputs. It requires a clear understanding of the task or problem being solved, identification of key inputs and outputs, and the ability to design prompts that accurately convey the intended meaning.

In addition to the tips mentioned earlier, there are other factors to consider in prompt engineering. For instance, it is important to understand the audience for whom the prompts are intended. Different audiences may require different levels of technicality or language usage, and tailoring the prompts accordingly can enhance communication and comprehension.

Furthermore, incorporating relevant domain-specific knowledge into prompts can significantly improve the AI's ability to generate accurate and contextually appropriate responses. By providing specific details or industry-specific terminology, the prompts can guide the AI towards generating outputs that align with the expected standards.

Prompt engineering also involves considering the context in which the prompts will be used. Whether it's in chatbots, language translation, or image generation, understanding the context helps in designing prompts that effectively communicate the desired outcomes. By aligning the prompts with the specific use case, we can enhance the AI's ability to generate responses that meet the needs and expectations of users.

It is worth noting that prompt engineering is an iterative process. It is important to continuously iterate on prompt design based on user feedback and performance metrics. By incorporating feedback from real users, we can identify areas where prompts may be unclear or ineffective and make necessary improvements. This iterative approach allows for continuous refinement and improvement in the overall effectiveness of the AI model.

In conclusion, prompt engineering is a vital component in the development of AI models that can generate high-quality outputs. By designing precise and robust prompts, we can effectively guide the AI's decision-making and ensure that the generated responses align with our intentions and objectives. The RGB prompt language model, along with other prompt engineering techniques, provides a structured approach to crafting prompts and enhancing the overall performance of AI models.

In the upcoming chapters, we will further explore prompt engineering techniques, delve into specific examples across different domains, and provide practical insights on how to apply prompt engineering effectively. So, let's continue our journey into the world of prompt engineering and unlock the full potential of AI.

CHAPTER 6: FUNDAMENTALS OF PROMPT ENGINEERING EXERCISE

1. Explain the role of prompts in language models.

2. Discuss the challenges of crafting effective prompts.

3. Experiment with different prompts using an AI language model like GPT-3.

CHAPTER 7
UNDERSTANDING PROMPT ENGINEERING

What is prompt engineering in a few words?

Prompt engineering is the process of creating instructions for AI tools or large language models (LLMs) such as ChatGPT and Google Bard, so that they can generate text, translate languages, write different kinds of creative content, and answer your questions in an informative way.

Prompt engineering is a fundamental concept in the field of artificial intelligence, particularly in the realm of natural language processing (NLP). It involves designing and generating prompts that effectively communicate the task or problem to be solved by the AI model. In this chapter, we will delve into the intricacies of prompt engineering, exploring its significance and various techniques.

One of the key aspects of prompt engineering is embedding the task description in the AI input. The prompts serve as instructions to guide the AI's decision-making process and generate the desired output. By carefully selecting the words and phrases used in the prompts, we can elicit precise and accurate responses from the AI model.

To understand the importance of prompt engineering, let's consider examples of good prompts and bad prompts. A poor prompt may be something like "Translate this sentence to French," which lacks specific information. In contrast, a good prompt would be "Please translate the following sentence into French: 'I would like to order a coffee and a croissant.'" The latter prompt provides clear instructions and specific details, ensuring that the AI understands the intended translation accurately.

The significance of specificity in prompts cannot be overstated. A vague or poorly constructed prompt can lead to ambiguity, making it difficult for the AI model to comprehend the task at hand. By providing specific information and instructions, we enable the AI to generate more accurate and relevant responses.

Let's explore the introduction of the Role Goal Benefit (RGB) prompt language model. Derived from the concept of user stories, the RGB model offers a structured approach to prompt design. It provides a framework for crafting prompts that include the role, goal, and benefit, thereby enhancing the precision and effectiveness of AI interactions.

In the RGB model, prompts are designed by framing them as user stories. For example, imagine you are a sales representative for a software company. Your goal is to sell a new project management software to a potential customer, with the benefit of increased productivity.

Using the RGB model, you would structure your prompt as follows: "As a sales representative for a software company, your goal is to sell our new project management software to a potential customer. By doing so, you will help increase their productivity and streamline their project management processes, leading to more efficient and effective project delivery."

By employing the RGB model, you provide the AI model with a clear understanding of your role, the desired outcome, and the benefits associated with achieving that outcome. This structured approach enables the AI to generate responses that align with your intentions and objectives.

The RGB prompt language model is particularly effective in guiding the AI's decision-making process. It helps set the context and provides a roadmap for the AI to follow, ensuring that the generated responses align with the specific goals and benefits outlined in the prompts.

The power of prompt engineering lies in its ability to make AI models more precise and accurate in their outputs. By using the RGB model or similar structured prompt formats, we can enhance the AI's understanding of the desired task and ensure that it generates responses that meet our expectations.

In the upcoming chapters, we will explore more examples and techniques for prompt engineering, covering different types of prompts, such as direct prompts and prompts by example. We will also discuss the importance of active verbs, the incorporation of domain-specific knowledge, and the consideration of the audience and context in prompt design.

Prompt engineering is a crucial skill for AI practitioners and developers. By mastering the art of prompt engineering, we can effectively harness the capabilities of AI models, automate tasks, and improve decision-making processes. So, let's delve deeper into the world of prompt engineering and unlock the full potential of AI-driven solutions.

RGB Relevance

Prompt engineering is a vital aspect of developing effective AI models that can generate high-quality outputs. By embedding the task description in the AI input and using well-crafted prompts, we can guide the AI's decision-making process and ensure that it produces the desired responses.

One of the key considerations in prompt engineering is the specificity of the prompts. Specific prompts provide clear instructions and guidelines to the AI, enabling it to generate accurate and relevant outputs. On the other hand, vague or ambiguous prompts can lead to confusion and produce inaccurate or irrelevant responses.

The Role Goal Benefit (RGB) prompt language model introduces a structured approach to prompt design, inspired by the concept of user stories. The RGB model encompasses the role, goal, and benefit within the prompts, allowing for more precise and effective communication with the AI models.

The RGB model prompts are framed as user stories, which outline the role of the user, their specific goal, and the associated benefit. By structuring prompts in this manner, we provide the AI with a clear understanding of the context and purpose of the task, leading to more accurate and aligned responses.

Let's delve deeper into the benefits of using the RGB prompt language model. By incorporating the role of the user, we establish the context and define the perspective from which the AI should approach the task. This ensures that the AI understands the specific role it needs to emulate or support.

The goal component of the RGB model prompts outlines the desired outcome or objective of the task. By clearly defining the goal, we guide the AI's decision-making process and align its responses with the intended purpose.

Lastly, the benefit aspect of the prompts highlights the positive outcomes or advantages associated with achieving the specified goal. By emphasizing the benefits, we provide the AI with a deeper understanding of the value it should strive to deliver.

The RGB model prompts help to eliminate ambiguity and ensure that the AI remains focused on the intended task. They provide a structured framework that enhances the precision and effectiveness of the AI's responses. By employing this model, we can streamline the AI-human interaction, leading to more efficient and accurate outputs.

In addition to the RGB model, prompt engineering encompasses various techniques and considerations. For example, the use of active verbs in prompts adds energy and urgency, driving the AI to respond accordingly. Incorporating domain-specific knowledge in prompts helps align the AI's responses with the specific requirements and expectations of the given domain.

Furthermore, considering the context in which the prompts will be used is essential. Different contexts may require different prompt designs and language usage. By tailoring prompts to the specific context, we can enhance the AI's ability to generate relevant and meaningful outputs.

Testing prompts with real users and gathering feedback is a crucial part of prompt engineering. This iterative process allows us to identify any areas where prompts may be unclear or ineffective and make improvements accordingly. By continuously refining prompt design based on user feedback and performance metrics, we can enhance the overall effectiveness of the AI model.

In the upcoming chapters, we will explore more examples and techniques of prompt engineering, covering different types of prompts such as direct prompts and prompts by example. We will also discuss the considerations of audience and context in prompt design and provide practical insights for effectively applying prompt engineering in various scenarios.

Prompt engineering is a powerful tool in the AI practitioner's toolkit. By understanding the significance of precise and well-structured prompts, we can leverage AI models to automate tasks, enhance decision-making, and achieve more accurate and aligned outcomes. So, let's continue our journey into the world of prompt engineering and unlock the full potential of AI-driven solutions.

CHAPTER 7: UNDERSTANDING PROMPT ENGINEERING EXERCISE

1. Explain the concept of temperature in prompt engineering.

2. Discuss the trade-offs in using more specific or more vague prompts.

3. Experiment with different prompt parameters such as temperature and max tokens using GPT-3.

CHAPTER 8
EXPLORING THE RGB MODEL

Prompt engineering forms the backbone of effective AI interactions, ensuring that the AI models generate precise and relevant outputs. In this chapter, we will delve deeper into the Role-Goal-Benefit Benefit (RGB) prompt language model, which derives its structure from user stories. We will explore how the RGB model can be applied to different roles and demonstrate its effectiveness in generating the desired outputs.

The RGB model provides a structured approach to prompt design, incorporating the elements of role, goal, and benefit. It allows us to clearly define the context, objectives, and advantages associated with a particular task. By framing prompts using the RGB model, we can enhance the AI's understanding and guide its decision-making process.

Let's examine some examples of prompts using the RGB model for different roles to gain a better understanding of its application and effectiveness.

1. Sales Representative Prompt: As a sales representative for a software company, your goal is to sell our new project management software to a potential customer. By doing so, you will help increase their productivity and streamline their project management processes, leading to more efficient and effective project delivery.

In this prompt, the role is defined as a sales representative, the goal is to sell the project management software, and the benefit is increased productivity and streamlined project management processes. By providing this clear and specific prompt, the AI can generate responses that align with the objectives of the sales representative.

2. Teacher Prompt: As a primary school teacher, your goal is to introduce a new interactive learning tool to your students. By doing so, you will increase student engagement and create an environment conducive to

improved learning outcomes. Incorporating this tool into the classroom will enhance student participation and motivation, leading to improved academic performance.

In this prompt, the role is that of a primary school teacher, the goal is to introduce an interactive learning tool, and the benefit is increased student engagement and improved learning outcomes. The prompt provides a comprehensive description of the teacher's objectives, allowing the AI to generate responses that support the desired educational outcomes.

3. Marketing Manager Prompt: As a marketing manager for a retail brand, your goal is to launch our new clothing line for the upcoming season. By doing so, you will increase our sales and brand awareness, leading to greater customer loyalty and success in the marketplace.

In this prompt, the role is that of a marketing manager, the goal is to launch a new clothing line, and the benefit is increased sales and brand awareness. The prompt highlights the marketing manager's objectives and the desired outcomes, enabling the AI to generate responses that align with the marketing goals.

4. Project Manager Prompt: As a project manager for a construction firm, your goal is to complete our new

building project on time and within budget. By doing so, you will satisfy our clients and increase our reputation in the industry, leading to more business opportunities and continued success.

In this prompt, the role is that of a project manager, the goal is to complete a building project on time and within budget, and the benefit is client satisfaction and enhanced reputation. The prompt provides a clear roadmap for the AI, enabling it to generate responses that address the project manager's objectives and the desired outcomes.

The RGB model prompts assist in generating the desired outputs by providing a precise and structured framework for the AI to follow. By defining the role, goal, and benefit within the prompts, we guide the AI's decision-making process and align its responses with the intended purpose.

The RGB model prompts help eliminate ambiguity and ensure that the AI remains focused on the desired task. They provide the necessary context and objectives, enabling the AI to generate responses that align with the intended outcomes. The structured nature of the prompts enhances the precision and effectiveness of the AI's outputs.

The WIFM Factor (What's in it for Me)

By incorporating the RGB model into prompt engineering, we can streamline the AI interaction and improve the quality of generated outputs. The RGB model acts as a guiding framework for prompt design, enabling AI models to understand the desired role, goal, and benefit associated with a given task.

When we apply the RGB model, we provide the AI with a clear understanding of the context and purpose of the prompt. This clarity helps the AI generate more accurate and contextually relevant responses. By incorporating the role, goal, and benefit within the prompt, we establish a strong foundation for the AI's decision-making process.

The RGB model is particularly effective because it draws inspiration from user stories, which are widely used in the agile development process. User stories capture the requirements, objectives, and benefits of a feature or task from the perspective of an end-user. By structuring prompts as user stories, we can effectively communicate the desired outcomes and guide the AI model in generating appropriate responses.

The power of the RGB model lies in its ability to provide a comprehensive and structured prompt that encapsulates the essential information needed for the AI model to generate relevant outputs. It ensures that the AI understands the role it needs to emulate, the specific goal it should strive to achieve, and the benefits associated with accomplishing that goal.

Moreover, the RGB model facilitates effective communication between humans and AI systems. By aligning the prompts with the user's perspective, it creates a shared understanding between the user and the AI model. This shared understanding helps establish a smoother and more efficient interaction, leading to more accurate and satisfying outcomes.

The Power of Specificity

In practice, using the RGB model prompts involves careful consideration of the specific role, goal, and benefit associated with a task. The prompts should be clear, concise, and focused on the most critical aspects of the task. The more precise and detailed the prompts are, the better the AI model can understand and generate outputs that meet the intended objectives.

For instance, let's consider the role of a sales representative. The prompt for the AI model could be structured as follows:

"As a sales representative for a software company, your goal is to sell our new project management software to a potential customer. By doing so, you will help increase their productivity and streamline their project management processes, leading to more efficient and effective project delivery."

In this prompt, the role is clearly defined as a sales representative. The goal is to sell the new project management software, and the benefit is increased productivity and streamlined project management processes. By providing this prompt, the AI model can understand the specific context and generate responses that align with the sales representative's objectives.

Similarly, prompts for other roles like teachers, marketing managers, and project managers can follow the same structure. The key is to provide a comprehensive description of the role, goal, and benefit, enabling the AI model to generate responses that support the desired outcomes.

The RGB model also helps in generating desired outputs by ensuring that the AI remains focused on the specific task at hand. With clear and well-defined prompts, the AI can understand the context and purpose of the task, avoiding potential confusion or ambiguity.

Furthermore, the RGB model allows for customization and adaptability. The prompts can be tailored to specific domains, industries, or even individual preferences. By incorporating domain-specific knowledge, terminology, and industry-specific goals, the prompts can guide the AI model to generate more accurate and relevant outputs.

Image Generation

The RGB model's effectiveness is not limited to text-based prompts. It can also be applied to other types of tasks, such as image generation. For example, a prompt for generating an image could be:

"Generate an image of a white Persian cat sitting on a windowsill, looking out at the moonlit city skyline."

In this prompt, the RGB model is still applicable. The role is to generate an image, the goal is to depict a white Persian cat on a windowsill, and the benefit is the visual aesthetics and emotional appeal of the moonlit city skyline. By providing such specific prompts, we guide the AI model in producing images that align with our expectations.

The RGB model's effectiveness can be further enhanced by incorporating additional instructions or constraints within the prompts. For example, we can specify the style, subject matter, or visual characteristics desired in the generated image. This level of detail ensures that the AI model understands our specific requirements and can produce outputs that meet those requirements.

It is important to note that prompt engineering is not limited to the RGB model alone. There are various other techniques and considerations involved in designing effective prompts. Direct prompts, for instance, explicitly instruct the AI model on what to do or what information to provide. Examples of direct prompts include asking the AI to translate a sentence to French or generate an image of a specific object.

On the other hand, prompts by example involve providing specific instances or samples to guide the AI model's generation process. For instance, asking the AI to generate a story based on a given set of characters, settings, and events is an example of a prompt by example. These techniques can be combined with the RGB model to create even more precise and robust prompts.

The Importance of Good Crafting

To illustrate the importance of specific and well-crafted prompts, let's consider some examples of good prompts versus bad prompts. A poor prompt may be something like, "Translate this sentence to French," without providing any sentence to translate. This prompt lacks the necessary information for the AI model to generate a meaningful response. In contrast, a good prompt would be, "Please translate the following sentence into French: 'I would like to order a coffee and a croissant.'"

Similarly, a vague prompt like "Write a short story" leaves room for interpretation and may result in a story that does not meet the desired requirements. In contrast, a good prompt would be, "Write a 500-word short story that includes the following three elements: a red balloon, a deserted beach, and a mysterious stranger." This prompt provides specific guidelines for the AI model to follow, resulting in a more focused and relevant story.

Prompt engineering is a continuous process that involves testing and iterating on the prompts based on user feedback and performance metrics. By gathering insights from real users, we can identify areas where the prompts may be unclear or ineffective and make improvements accordingly. This iterative approach helps refine the prompt design and enhance the overall effectiveness of the AI model.

In conclusion, prompt engineering plays a crucial role in AI systems, particularly in natural language processing tasks. The RGB prompt language model provides a structured framework for designing effective prompts by incorporating the elements of role, goal, and benefit. By using this model and other techniques like direct prompts and prompts by example, we can guide the AI model's decision-making process and generate desired outputs.

The RGB model's ability to generate precise and robust prompts ensures that the AI understands the context, objectives, and benefits associated with a given task. This, in turn, leads to more accurate, relevant, and aligned responses. Prompt engineering, when done effectively, enables us to leverage the full potential of AI models, automate tasks, and enhance decision-making processes.

In the next chapter, we will explore practical examples and applications of prompt engineering in different domains and scenarios. We will dive deeper into the process of designing and generating prompts, considering the audience, context, and specific requirements of each task. So, let's continue our journey into the world of prompt engineering and uncover the limitless possibilities of AI-driven solutions.

CHAPTER 8: EXPLORING THE RGB MODEL EXERCISE

1. Explain the role of RGB in image processing.

2. Discuss how the RGB model represents color.

3. Write a program that can manipulate the RGB values of an image to apply different filters.

CHAPTER 9
RGB MODEL DETAILS

The RGB (Role, Goal, Benefit) model has emerged as a powerful framework for understanding and optimizing various aspects of industries and processes. With its ability to delineate the fundamental roles, define specific goals, and uncover the associated benefits, the RGB model has become a cornerstone of effective analysis and decision-making.

In this chapter, we embark on a comprehensive exploration of the RGB model, delving into its intricacies and applications across different industries. Through a deep dive into this model, we aim to unravel its inner workings, showcasing its versatility and potential for driving success.

Throughout these pages, we will examine how the RGB model can be leveraged to guide strategic planning, project management, and problem-solving in a wide array of contexts. We will explore how organizations define and refine their roles within their industries, establish clear and measurable goals, and ultimately reap the benefits of their endeavors.

From business and marketing to technology and healthcare, we will dive into diverse industries to uncover how the RGB model serves as a guiding framework. We will examine real-world examples where organizations have successfully employed this model to optimize their operations, improve customer satisfaction, and achieve their desired outcomes.

By understanding the distinct roles that different entities play within their respective industries, we can effectively identify the goals they strive to achieve. With a clear understanding of these goals, we can then explore the various strategies and actions that can be taken to attain the desired benefits through intentional and effective prompt engineering with the RGB model.

Section 1: Role in Prompt Engineering

The first component of the RGB Prompt Language Model is the Role. The Role defines the position or persona that the AI is meant to embody or simulate. It provides a clear context and sets the stage for the AI's understanding of the task at hand. In this section, we will delve into the role component of the prompt, exploring how to state it effectively.

I. Defining the Prompt Role When stating the prompt role, it is essential to provide specific details about the role's characteristics and responsibilities. Consider the following points when formulating the prompt role:

1. Specify the Job Title or Position: Clearly state the job title or position that the AI is representing. For example, "As a sales representative," "As a primary school teacher," or "As a marketing manager."

2. Describe the Domain or Industry: Provide information about the domain or industry to further contextualize the role. For instance, "As a sales representative for a software company" or "As a marketing manager for a retail brand."

3. Highlight Relevant Expertise or Experience: Mention any relevant expertise or experience that the role possesses. For example, "With 14 years of experience

on large I.T. hardware projects" or "Experienced in launching new clothing lines for the upcoming season."

II. Importance of the Role Component The role component is crucial in prompt engineering as it sets the context and frames the AI's perspective. By defining a specific role, we guide the AI's decision-making process and ensure that the generated outputs align with the intended objectives of that role.

III. Example of Role Component As an example, let's consider the role of a project manager for a construction firm. The prompt could begin as follows: "As a project manager for a construction firm, your goal is to complete our new building project on time and within budget..."

Section 2: Goal in Prompt Engineering

The second component of the RGB Prompt Language Model is the Goal. The Goal defines the specific objective or task that the AI is expected to accomplish. It provides clarity and direction to the AI, guiding its decision-making process. In this section, we will explore how to state the prompt goal effectively.

I. Defining the Prompt Goal When stating the prompt goal, it is essential to be precise and focused on the desired outcome. Consider the following points when formulating the prompt goal:

1. Identify the Objective: Clearly articulate the objective or task that the AI needs to achieve. For example, "your goal is to sell our new project management software," "your goal is to introduce a new interactive learning tool to your students," or "your goal is to launch our new clothing line for the upcoming season."

2. Be Specific and Measurable: State the goal in a way that is specific and measurable. Avoid vague or ambiguous language. For instance, instead of saying "increase sales," specify the target, such as "increase sales by 20%."

3. Consider Timeframes or Deadlines: If applicable, include timeframes or deadlines for achieving the goal. This adds an additional level of specificity and urgency. For example, "complete our new building project on time and within budget."

II. Importance of the Goal Component The goal component plays a crucial role in prompt engineering as it defines the purpose and objective of the AI's actions. By stating a clear and specific goal, we guide the AI's decision-making towards generating outputs that align with achieving that goal.

III. Example of Goal Component Continuing with the example of a project manager, the prompt could state the goal as follows: "...your goal is to complete our new building project on time and within budget by coordinating resources and ensuring efficient project management."

Section 3: Benefit in Prompt Engineering

The third component of the RGB Prompt Language Model is the Benefit. The Benefit highlights the positive outcomes, advantages, or value that will be derived from achieving the prompt goal. It provides motivation and purpose to the AI, reinforcing the significance of the task. In this section, we will explore how to state the prompt benefit effectively.

I. Defining the Prompt Benefit When stating the prompt benefit, it is important to emphasize the positive impact or value that will result from accomplishing the goal. Consider the following points when formulating the prompt benefit:

1. Identify the Positive Outcome: Clearly articulate the positive outcome or benefit that will be derived from achieving the goal. For example, "by doing so, you will help increase their productivity and streamline their project management processes," or "leading to greater customer loyalty and success in the marketplace."

2. Highlight the Value or Impact: Describe the value or impact that the desired outcome will have on the stakeholders or the organization. This could include increased efficiency, improved performance, cost

savings, enhanced customer satisfaction, or other relevant benefits.

3. Make it Relevant and Compelling: Ensure that the stated benefit is relevant to the context and meaningful to the role. It should be compelling enough to motivate the AI to strive towards accomplishing the goal.

II. Importance of the Benefit Component The benefit component is crucial in prompt engineering as it reinforces the purpose and significance of the task. By highlighting the positive outcomes or value associated with achieving the goal, we provide the AI with a sense of purpose and encourage it to generate outputs that align with delivering those benefits.

III. Example of Benefit Component Taking the example of a project manager, the prompt could state the benefit as follows: "...leading to more business opportunities and continued success by satisfying our clients and increasing our reputation in the industry."

By combining the role, goal, and benefit components within the prompt, we provide the AI with a comprehensive understanding of the task at hand. The role establishes the context, the goal defines the objective, and the benefit reinforces the positive outcomes. This structured approach enables the AI to generate outputs that align with the intended objectives and deliver value to the stakeholders.

In conclusion, the RGB Prompt Language Model's Role - Goal - Benefit framework is a powerful tool in prompt engineering. By clearly defining the role, goal, and benefit within the prompts, we guide the AI's decision-making process and ensure that the generated outputs are precise, relevant, and aligned with the desired outcomes. Understanding how to state each component effectively allows us to leverage the full potential of the AI models and drive successful interactions and outcomes.

CHAPTER 9: RGB MODEL DETAILS EXERCISE

1. Discuss the limitations of the RGB model in the context of AI creativity.

2. How would you overcome such limitations?

3. Does the RGB model apply to image generation? Why or why not do you think so?

CHAPTER 10
DEEPENING RGB MODEL UNDERSTANDING

Prompt engineering plays a pivotal role in designing effective AI models that can generate high-quality outputs. In this chapter, we will delve deeper into the significance of prompt engineering and explore its application in various tasks, including language generation and image generation. Additionally, we will examine examples of prompts that incorporate specific task requirements and characteristics. Furthermore, we will discuss the importance of considering relevant fields, axes, and phrases in prompts and how to incorporate data from different sources such as CSV files, images, and HTML.

1. Role of Prompt Engineering in Designing Effective AI Models: Prompt engineering serves as a crucial component in the design of AI models. It involves crafting prompts that effectively guide the decision-making process of the AI model. The prompts act as instructions, providing the necessary context and guidelines for the AI model to generate the desired output. By employing effective prompt engineering techniques, AI models can produce outputs that align with the specific objectives and requirements of the given task.

2. Prompt Engineering for Language Generation and Image Generation Tasks: Prompt engineering is applicable to various tasks, including both language generation and image generation. In language generation tasks, prompts are designed to convey the desired meaning, tone, and style of the generated text. They can include specific instructions, keywords, or examples that guide the AI model in producing coherent and contextually relevant responses. Similarly, in image generation tasks, prompts are tailored to

specify the desired style, subject matter, or visual characteristics of the generated image. By providing precise prompts, AI models can generate images that align with the intended requirements.

- Examples of Prompts for Specific Tasks and Characteristics: Let's explore some examples of prompts that demonstrate the application of prompt engineering in specific tasks and characteristics. For instance, in language generation, a prompt could be:
  - ○ ROLE: As a marketing copywriter,
  - ○ GOAL: I want to create a persuasive product description,
  - ○ BENEFIT: In such a way that it captivates the target audience and drives sales.

This prompt clearly defines the role, goal, and benefit, providing the AI model with the necessary context to generate compelling product descriptions.

In image generation, a prompt could be:

- ○ ROLE: As a concept artist
- ○ GOAL: I need to design a futuristic cityscape
- ○ BENEFIT: In such a way that it showcases advanced technology and a sense of grandeur.

This prompt conveys the specific role, goal, and

desired benefits, guiding the AI model to create an image that captures the futuristic essence and desired visual elements.

4. Consideration of Relevant Fields, Axes, and Phrases in Prompts: To enhance the specificity and precision of prompts, it is essential to consider relevant fields, axes, and phrases that are pertinent to the given task. For example, when generating text for data analysis, prompts could include specific variables, statistical measures, or analysis techniques to be applied. In image generation, prompts may mention color palettes, composition rules, or visual themes to guide the AI model in producing the desired visual output. By incorporating such details, prompts become more targeted, leading to more accurate and relevant results.

5. Incorporating Data in Prompts (CSV, Images, HTML, etc.): Prompt engineering allows for the incorporation of various data formats into prompts, such as CSV files, images, HTML, and more. This capability enables the AI model to leverage external data sources and incorporate them into its decision-making process. For example, a prompt for data analysis could involve referencing a specific CSV file containing relevant datasets. In image generation, prompts may include

references to images or visual inspirations to guide the AI model in creating the desired visual output. By incorporating data in prompts, AI models can generate outputs that are informed by real-world data and align with specific requirements.

In conclusion, prompt engineering is a vital aspect of designing effective AI models. It involves crafting prompts that serve as instructions to guide the decision-making process of AI models. By applying prompt engineering techniques, we can tailor prompts for language generation and image generation tasks to ensure the desired outcomes.

In language generation, prompts should clearly define the role, goal, and benefit of the task at hand. This helps the AI model understand the specific context and generate text that aligns with the intended purpose. By providing examples, keywords, or specific instructions, we guide the AI model to produce coherent and relevant responses.

Similarly, in image generation, prompts play a crucial role in specifying the desired style, subject matter, and visual characteristics of the generated image. By incorporating precise details such as color palettes, composition rules, or visual themes, we guide the AI model to create images that meet the specific requirements.

To make prompts more effective, it is important to consider relevant fields, axes, and phrases that are specific to the task. By including these details, we provide the AI model with the necessary context and guide its decision-making process more precisely. This leads to more accurate and relevant outputs.

Prompt engineering also allows for the incorporation of external data sources into prompts. By referencing CSV files, images, HTML, or other data formats, we can enhance the AI model's understanding and decision-making process. This enables the model to leverage real-world data and generate outputs that are informed by the provided data.

The advantage of writing prompts using the Role - Goal - Benefit model and incorporating specific details and data is that it helps to generate more precise and targeted outputs. By clearly defining the role, goal, and benefit, we provide the AI model with a comprehensive understanding of the task and guide it towards producing the desired outcomes. This approach improves the overall effectiveness and efficiency of prompt engineering.

Prompts for Tables

Generating prompts for data in tables requires careful consideration of the specific requirements and desired presentation format. The RGB model can be effectively utilized to craft prompts that precisely instruct the AI model to generate the desired table outputs. Here are some major rules to keep in mind when generating prompts for table data:

1. Clearly Define the Table Structure: Clearly specify the table's structure, including the number of rows and columns, headers, and any special formatting requirements. This ensures that the AI model understands the intended layout of the table.

Example: ROLE: As a data analyst, GOAL: Create a table with 5 rows and 4 columns displaying monthly sales data, BENEFIT: to analyze trends and identify top-selling products.

2. Specify Data Fields and Formats: Specify the fields of data required in the table and the desired formats, such as numerical values, dates, or text. This helps the AI model populate the table with the relevant data.

Example: ROLE: As a marketing manager, GOAL: Generate a table with customer demographics, including age, gender, and location, BENEFIT: to analyze target market segments for campaign planning.

3. Define Sorting and Filtering Criteria: If sorting or filtering is necessary, provide clear instructions on the criteria and the order in which the data should be sorted. This helps the AI model arrange the data in the desired manner.

Example: ROLE: As a financial analyst, GOAL: Generate a table of stocks sorted by market capitalization in descending order, BENEFIT: to identify top-performing companies in the market.

4. Incorporate Aggregation and Summarization: If you require aggregated or summarized data in the table, specify the calculations or metrics to be applied to the data.

Example: ROLE: As a project manager, GOAL: Create a table summarizing project progress by displaying the total tasks completed, pending tasks, and percentage of completion for each team, BENEFIT: to monitor project status at a glance.

5. Request Data Grouping: If you need data to be grouped based on specific criteria, provide instructions on the grouping parameters to achieve a meaningful representation of the data.

Example: ROLE: As a sales team lead, GOAL: Generate a table grouping sales data by product category and displaying total revenue for each category, BENEFIT: to identify the most profitable product categories.

6. Formatting and Styling Instructions: If specific formatting or styling is required, such as font type, font size, borders, or colors, provide explicit instructions to ensure the table's visual presentation meets your expectations.

Example: ROLE: As a designer, GOAL: Create a visually appealing table displaying color swatches, including HEX codes and corresponding RGB values, BENEFIT: to assist in color selection for design projects.

7. Request Multiple Tables or Subtables: If you require multiple tables or subtables within a larger context, clearly state the relationships and organization of the tables to convey the desired hierarchical structure.

Example: ROLE: As a project coordinator, GOAL: Generate a project timeline table with separate subtables for each phase, including start and end dates, milestones, and responsible teams, BENEFIT: to provide a comprehensive overview of the project's timeline.

By adhering to these rules, you can effectively utilize the RGB model to generate prompts that guide the AI model in creating tables with the desired data representation and formatting. Whether it's CSV, HTML, JPG, tree structures, or other formats, the RGB model combined with precise prompt engineering enables you to obtain accurate and structured tabular outputs tailored to your specific needs.

The RGB prompt engineering model is a powerful technique that allows us to guide AI models in generating accurate and relevant outputs. By carefully crafting prompts that incorporate specific details, data, and follow the Role - Goal - Benefit model, we can optimize the performance of AI models in language and image generation tasks. Through effective prompt engineering, we can harness the true potential of AI technology and achieve remarkable results in various industries and applications.

CHAPTER 10: DEEPENING RGB MODEL UNDERSTANDING EXERCISE

1. Discuss the benefits of using the RGB model in project management.
2. Create an example of an RGB prompt for a hypothetical project or task. If stuck, ask Google Bard or ChatGPT!

CHAPTER 11
PRACTICAL EXAMPLES AND APPLICATIONS

Prompt engineering is a powerful tool that can be applied in various scenarios to generate compelling arguments, design informative views, and create efficient project backlogs. In this chapter, we will explore practical examples and applications of prompt engineering, showcasing its effectiveness in different contexts.

1. Generating a Compelling Argument for Infrastructure Refresh: Prompt engineering can be used to craft a persuasive argument for infrastructure refresh. By employing the Role - Goal - Benefit model, we can

create prompts that clearly define the role, goal, and benefit of the task. For example, "ROLE: As a system administrator, GOAL: I would like to rear range and optimize the existing infrastructure, BENEFIT: in such a way that it improves overall performance, reduces downtime, and enhances scalability." By formulating prompts in this manner, we provide the AI model with a concise and focused understanding of the desired outcome, enabling it to generate a compelling argument that highlights the benefits of infrastructure refresh.

2. Designing a Tabular View with Pros and Cons for Hardware and Software Upgrade: Prompt engineering can also be applied to design informative views, such as tabular formats with pros and cons. For instance,

- "ROLE: As a technology consultant,
- GOAL: I need to present a comprehensive analysis of hardware and software upgrade options,
- BENEFIT: in such a way that it facilitates informed decision-making." By providing this prompt, we guide the AI model to generate a tabular view that outlines the advantages and disadvantages of different upgrade options, allowing

stakeholders to make informed choices based on the presented information.

3. Creating a Product Backlog for a Windows Upgrade Project: Prompt engineering is instrumental in creating a well-structured product backlog for projects. For example, "ROLE: As a project manager, GOAL: I need to develop a product backlog for a Windows upgrade project, BENEFIT: in such a way that it prioritizes key features and aligns with the project objectives." By formulating this prompt, we guide the AI model to generate a product backlog that captures the essential features, tasks, and priorities necessary for a successful Windows upgrade project.

4. Leveraging the Power of Prompt Engineering in Different Scenarios: Prompt engineering can be applied in various other scenarios, catering to different industries and domains. Let's consider a few examples:

   a. Sales and Marketing: "ROLE: As a sales representative, GOAL: I aim to create a persuasive sales pitch, BENEFIT: in such a way that it drives customer engagement, boosts conversion rates, and increases revenue."

   b. Healthcare: "ROLE: As a medical researcher, GOAL: I seek to analyze patient data, BENEFIT: in such a way that it identifies patterns, aids in diagnosis, and contributes to advancements in treatment."

c. Science: "ROLE: As a scientist, GOAL: I want to design an experiment, BENEFIT: in such a way that it validates hypotheses, generates reliable data, and advances scientific knowledge."

d. Automotive: "ROLE: As an automotive engineer, GOAL: I aim to develop an energy-efficient vehicle, BENEFIT: in such a way that it reduces emissions, improves fuel efficiency, and promotes sustainable transportation."

e. Mechanical Engineering: "ROLE: As a mechanical engineer, GOAL: I need to optimize the design of a mechanical component, BENEFIT: in such a way that it enhances performance, reduces weight, and increases reliability."

f. Chemical Engineering: "ROLE: As a chemical engineer, GOAL: I seek to develop a more efficient production process, BENEFIT: in such a way that it minimizes waste, maximizes yield, and improves cost-effectiveness."

In each of these examples, prompt engineering empowers AI models to generate outputs that align with our requirements.

The advantage of prompt engineering lies in its ability to streamline and optimize various processes. By providing clear instructions, incorporating relevant details, and following the Role - Goal - Benefit framework, prompt engineering ensures that AI models understand the task at hand and generate outputs that are precise, relevant, and aligned with the desired outcomes.

Furthermore, prompt engineering helps in improving efficiency and reducing the time and effort required to accomplish complex tasks. By leveraging the power of AI, prompt engineering allows us to automate processes, generate reports, and create comprehensive deliverables with speed and accuracy. This not only saves valuable time but also enhances productivity and enables us to focus on higher-value activities.

Moreover, prompt engineering enhances the interpretability and transparency of AI models. By structuring prompts that explicitly state the role, goal, and benefit, we create a clear framework for the AI model to follow. This facilitates better understanding and evaluation of the generated outputs, making it easier to validate the results and ensure they align with the intended objectives.

In conclusion, prompt engineering is a fundamental component in harnessing the capabilities of AI models. By carefully structuring prompts using the Role - Goal - Benefit model and incorporating specific details, we can guide AI models to generate outputs that are tailored to our requirements. With its ability to streamline processes, improve efficiency, and enhance interpretability, prompt engineering is a valuable technique that empowers us to leverage the full potential of AI technology in various industries and applications.

50 Examples of the RGB Model

1. Banking:

ROLE: As a financial analyst at a leading bank

GOAL: I need to analyze customer transaction data

BENEFIT: In such a way that we can identify patterns, detect anomalies, and enhance fraud detection measures.

2. Engineering:

ROLE: As a mechanical engineer in the aerospace industry

GOAL: I want to optimize the design of a propulsion system

BENEFIT: In such a way that we can achieve higher efficiency, reduce fuel consumption, and improve overall performance.

3. Commerce:

ROLE: As an e-commerce manager for an online marketplace

GOAL: I aim to improve the product recommendation algorithm

BENEFIT: In such a way that we can personalize user experiences, increase customer satisfaction, and boost sales conversion rates.

4. Marketing:

ROLE: As a marketing strategist for a global brand

GOAL: I want to analyze social media engagement metrics

BENEFIT: In such a way that we can gauge campaign effectiveness, identify target audience preferences, and optimize marketing strategies.

5. Sales:

ROLE: As a sales representative in the pharmaceutical industry

GOAL: I need to analyze customer feedback and sales data

BENEFIT: In such a way that we can identify market trends, enhance customer satisfaction, and tailor sales strategies to specific needs.

6. Healthcare:

ROLE: As a healthcare administrator in a hospital

GOAL: I aim to optimize patient scheduling and resource allocation

BENEFIT: In such a way that we can reduce waiting times, improve patient care, and enhance overall operational efficiency.

7. Science:

ROLE: As a research scientist in a biotechnology company

GOAL: I want to analyze genomic data

BENEFIT: In such a way that we can identify genetic markers, explore disease pathways, and advance medical research and treatments.

8. Automotive:

ROLE: As an automotive engineer for a leading car manufacturer

GOAL: I need to optimize vehicle safety features

BENEFIT: In such a way that we can enhance occupant protection, reduce accident risks, and improve overall vehicle safety ratings.

9. Mechanical Engineering:

ROLE: As a mechanical engineer specializing in renewable energy systems

GOAL: I aim to optimize the design of a wind turbine

BENEFIT: In such a way that we can increase energy generation efficiency, reduce maintenance costs, and promote sustainable energy production.

10. Chemical Engineering:

ROLE: As a chemical engineer in a pharmaceutical company

GOAL: I want to optimize the drug formulation process

BENEFIT: In such a way that we can improve product quality, ensure consistency, and enhance patient safety and efficacy.

11. Administration:

ROLE: As an administrator in a large organization

GOAL: I need to analyze employee productivity data

BENEFIT: In such a way that we can identify performance gaps, enhance resource allocation, and optimize workforce efficiency.

12. Communications:

ROLE: As a communications manager for a technology company

GOAL: I aim to analyze customer feedback and sentiment data

BENEFIT: In such a way that we can improve brand reputation, identify areas for improvement, and enhance customer satisfaction and loyalty.

13. Education:

ROLE: As an educational researcher in a university

GOAL: I want to analyze student performance data

BENEFIT: In such a way that we can identify effective teaching strategies, personalize education, and support student success.

14. Hospitality:

ROLE: As a hotel manager in a luxury resort

GOAL: I need to analyze customer reviews and feedback

BENEFIT: In such a way that we can enhance guest experiences, address concerns promptly, and improve overall customer

15. Aerospace:

ROLE: As an aerospace engineer at a space exploration agency

GOAL: I aim to optimize rocket propulsion systems

BENEFIT: In such a way that we can achieve higher thrust, reduce fuel consumption, and improve mission success rates.

16. Information Technology:

ROLE: As an IT manager in a large corporation

GOAL: I want to analyze network performance data

BENEFIT: In such a way that we can identify bottlenecks, enhance network efficiency, and ensure uninterrupted operations.

17. Environmental Science:

ROLE: As an environmental scientist in a research institute

GOAL: I need to analyze climate data from various sources

BENEFIT: In such a way that we can understand long-term trends, predict climate patterns, and develop effective mitigation strategies.

18. Retail:

ROLE: As a retail store manager

GOAL: I aim to analyze sales data and customer behavior

BENEFIT: In such a way that we can optimize inventory management, personalize marketing campaigns, and increase customer satisfaction.

19. Legal:

ROLE: As a legal researcher in a law firm

GOAL: I want to analyze case precedents and legal statutes

BENEFIT: In such a way that we can build stronger legal arguments, streamline legal research processes, and improve client representation.

20. Energy:

ROLE: As an energy analyst in a renewable energy company

GOAL: I need to analyze energy consumption patterns

BENEFIT: In such a way that we can identify energy-saving opportunities, promote sustainable practices, and reduce carbon emissions.

21. Agriculture:

ROLE: As an agricultural scientist at a research institution

GOAL: I aim to analyze soil composition and nutrient levels

BENEFIT: In such a way that we can optimize crop yields, improve resource management, and promote sustainable farming practices.

22. Tourism:

ROLE: As a tourism manager for a travel agency

GOAL: I want to analyze customer feedback and travel trends

BENEFIT: In such a way that we can personalize travel experiences, enhance customer satisfaction, and tailor offerings to specific preferences.

23. Entertainment:

ROLE: As an entertainment producer for a film production company

GOAL: I need to analyze audience preferences and box office performance

BENEFIT: In such a way that we can create engaging content, increase ticket sales, and ensure profitability for film releases.

24. Fashion:

ROLE: As a fashion designer for a luxury brand

GOAL: I aim to analyze consumer fashion trends and preferences

BENEFIT: In such a way that we can develop innovative designs, meet market demands, and increase brand loyalty.

25. Sports:

ROLE: As a sports analyst for a professional sports team

GOAL: I want to analyze player performance and team statistics

BENEFIT: In such a way that we can improve strategic decision-making, enhance training programs, and increase the team's chances of winning.

26. Food and Beverage:

ROLE: As a chef in a high-end restaurant

GOAL: I need to analyze customer feedback and menu preferences

BENEFIT: In such a way that we can create exceptional dining experiences, improve menu offerings, and increase customer satisfaction.

27. Real Estate:

ROLE: As a real estate agent for a property brokerage

GOAL: I aim to analyze market trends and property values

BENEFIT: In such a way that we can provide accurate property evaluations, assist clients in making informed investment decisions, and maximize returns.

28. Renewable Energy:

ROLE: As an energy engineer specializing in solar power

GOAL: I want to optimize the design of solar panel systems

BENEFIT: In such a way that we can increase energy generation efficiency, reduce carbon footprint, and promote clean and sustainable energy sources.

29. Education Technology:

ROLE: As an EdTech product manager

GOAL: I need to analyze student learning data and platform usability

BENEFIT: In such a way that we can enhance personalized learning experiences, improve educational outcomes, and empower students and teachers.

30. Pharmaceuticals:

ROLE: As a pharmaceutical researcher in a drug development company

GOAL: I aim to analyze clinical trial data and drug efficacy

BENEFIT: In such a way that we can advance medical treatments, improve patient outcomes, and contribute to better healthcare practices.

31. Telecommunications:

ROLE: As a telecommunications engineer for a telecommunications provider

GOAL: I want to analyze network performance and customer satisfaction data

BENEFIT: In such a way that we can optimize network reliability, enhance service quality, and ensure customer loyalty.

32. Non-Profit:

ROLE: As a program manager for a non-profit organization

GOAL: I need to analyze impact measurement data

BENEFIT: In such a way that we can demonstrate the effectiveness of our programs, secure funding, and make a positive difference in the lives of beneficiaries.

33. Automotive Manufacturing:

ROLE: As a quality control engineer in an automobile manufacturing plant

GOAL: I aim to analyze production line data and identify areas for improvement

BENEFIT: In such a way that we can enhance product quality, increase operational efficiency, and ensure customer satisfaction.

34. Environmental Conservation:

ROLE: As an environmental conservationist in a wildlife preservation organization

GOAL: I want to analyze biodiversity data and habitat trends

BENEFIT: In such a way that we can identify endangered species, protect critical habitats, and contribute to the preservation of ecosystems for future generations.

35. Logistics:

ROLE: As a supply chain manager for a global logistics company

GOAL: I aim to analyze transportation data and optimize delivery routes

BENEFIT: In such a way that we can reduce shipping costs, improve delivery times, and enhance overall supply chain efficiency.

36. Architecture:

ROLE: As an architect in a design firm

GOAL: I need to analyze building performance and energy efficiency

BENEFIT: In such a way that we can create sustainable and environmentally friendly designs, reduce energy consumption, and promote green building practices.

37. Hospitality Technology:

ROLE: As a technology consultant for the hospitality industry

GOAL: I want to analyze guest experience data and technology infrastructure

BENEFIT: In such a way that we can enhance guest satisfaction, streamline operations, and improve the overall efficiency of hospitality services.

38. Insurance:

ROLE: As an insurance claims adjuster

GOAL: I aim to analyze claims data and identify fraudulent activities

BENEFIT: In such a way that we can reduce fraudulent claims, minimize financial losses, and ensure fair and accurate claim settlements.

39. Human Resources:

ROLE: As an HR manager in a multinational corporation

GOAL: I need to analyze employee engagement and performance data

BENEFIT: In such a way that we can improve employee satisfaction, increase productivity, and foster a positive work culture.

40. Government:

ROLE: As a policy analyst in a government agency

GOAL: I want to analyze public opinion and policy effectiveness

BENEFIT: In such a way that we can shape evidence-based policies, enhance public trust, and ensure effective governance.

41. Education:

ROLE: As an instructional designer in an e-learning company

GOAL: I aim to develop interactive online courses

BENEFIT: In such a way that we can enhance learner engagement, improve knowledge retention, and facilitate effective remote learning.

42. Hospitality:

ROLE: As a hotel manager in a luxury resort

GOAL: I want to analyze guest feedback to enhance guest experiences

BENEFIT: In such a way that we can increase guest satisfaction, foster positive online reviews, and generate repeat business.

43. Retail:

ROLE: As a retail store manager in a fashion boutique

GOAL: I aim to analyze sales data and optimize inventory management

BENEFIT: In such a way that we can reduce stockouts, minimize excess inventory, and improve overall profitability.

44. Technology:

ROLE: As a cybersecurity analyst in an IT consulting firm

GOAL: I want to analyze network vulnerabilities and strengthen cybersecurity measures

BENEFIT: In such a way that we can protect sensitive data, mitigate security risks, and ensure business continuity.

45. Manufacturing:

ROLE: As a production supervisor in an automotive assembly plant

GOAL: I aim to analyze production line efficiency and minimize downtime

BENEFIT: In such a way that we can increase productivity, reduce costs, and improve overall manufacturing performance.

46. Consulting:

ROLE: As a management consultant in a strategic advisory firm

GOAL: I want to analyze market trends and competitive landscape

BENEFIT: In such a way that we can provide data-driven insights, identify growth opportunities, and guide strategic decision-making.

47. Energy:

ROLE: As an energy efficiency engineer in a renewable energy company

GOAL: I aim to analyze energy consumption patterns and identify optimization opportunities

BENEFIT: In such a way that we can reduce carbon footprint, lower energy costs, and promote sustainable energy practices.

48. Nonprofit:

ROLE: As a fundraising manager for a charitable organization

GOAL: I want to analyze donor engagement and optimize fundraising strategies

BENEFIT: In such a way that we can increase donations, support more impactful projects, and make a meaningful difference in the community.

49. Legal:

ROLE: As a legal researcher in a law firm

GOAL: I aim to analyze case precedents and legal statutes

BENEFIT: In such a way that we can provide accurate legal advice, strengthen legal arguments, and ensure favorable outcomes for clients.

50. Insurance:

ROLE: As an actuary in an insurance company

GOAL: I want to analyze risk factors and develop pricing models

BENEFIT: In such a way that we can ensure appropriate insurance premiums, minimize financial losses, and maintain the company's profitability.

These examples demonstrate how the RGB model can be applied across various industries. The Role component establishes the context and the specific position from which the prompt is generated. The Goal component defines the specific task or objective to be achieved, focusing on the analysis or optimization of data or systems. The Benefit component highlights the positive outcomes or value derived from accomplishing the goal, such as improved efficiency, cost savings, enhanced decision-making, or positive impact on stakeholders.

By structuring prompts in this format, we provide clear instructions to ChatGPT, enabling it to generate responses that align with the intended objectives. The RGB model ensures that prompts are concise, specific, and result-oriented, promoting effective prompt engineering and generating valuable outputs.

Benefit of the RGB Model

Let's review the advantages of writing prompts using the Role - Goal - Benefit (RGB) model:

1. Clear Communication and Context Setting: The RGB model serves as a powerful framework that enables clear communication and context setting with ChatGPT or any AI language model. By explicitly stating the Role, Goal, and Benefit components in your prompts, you provide the model with a solid understanding of the specific context, objectives, and desired outcomes. This clarity helps the AI model comprehend your intentions accurately, leading to more precise and relevant responses.

2. Enhanced Precision and Relevance: With the RGB model, you gain the ability to craft prompts that are not only concise but also highly specific and tailored to your needs. By clearly defining the Role, you establish the

perspective from which the prompt should be approached, allowing the AI model to simulate a particular professional or stakeholder's viewpoint. The Goal component provides a precise task or objective that the AI model should focus on, directing its attention towards the desired outcome. Finally, the Benefit component articulates the advantages or positive impact that you seek to achieve through the prompt, ensuring that the AI model understands the ultimate purpose behind the task. This level of specificity and precision in prompts significantly enhances the relevance and quality of the generated responses.

3. Efficient Prompt Engineering and Time Savings: Using the RGB model streamlines the prompt engineering process, enabling you to create prompts more efficiently and effectively. The clear structure of Role - Goal - Benefit guides your thinking and prompts you to consider the essential elements of a prompt. By following this model, you save valuable time and effort that would otherwise be spent in trial and error attempts to obtain desired outputs. The RGB model empowers you to express your requirements explicitly, reducing the need for iterative adjustments and fine-

tuning of prompts. This efficiency allows you to focus your energy on higher-level tasks and analysis rather than getting lost in the intricacies of prompt engineering.

4. Alignment with User's Intentions and Expectations: One of the key benefits of the RGB model is its ability to align the AI-generated outputs with the user's intentions and expectations. By clearly articulating the Role, Goal, and Benefit, you establish a shared understanding between yourself and the AI model. This alignment ensures that the generated responses are more likely to meet your specific requirements and deliver the desired outcomes. Whether you are seeking analysis, optimization, recommendations, or any other form of response, the RGB model acts as a guide to prompt the AI model towards providing information that aligns with your objectives.

In summary, the Role - Goal - Benefit (RGB) model offers significant advantages in prompt engineering by enabling clear communication, enhancing precision and relevance, streamlining the process, and aligning outputs with user intentions. By adopting this model, you unlock the true potential of AI language models like ChatGPT, leveraging their capabilities to generate responses that truly meet your needs.

Embrace the RGB model and embark on a journey of prompt engineering excellence, where precision, efficiency, and value converge to revolutionize your AI endeavors.

Prompt engineering can be applied in numerous industries and scenarios, allowing us to harness the power of AI technology to generate tailored outputs that meet specific objectives. By carefully structuring prompts using the Role - Goal - Benefit model, we provide the necessary guidance and context for AI models to generate outputs that align with our requirements.

The advantage of prompt engineering lies in its ability to streamline and optimize various processes. By providing clear instructions, incorporating relevant details, and following the Role - Goal - Benefit framework, prompt engineering ensures that AI models understand the task at hand and generate outputs that are precise, relevant, and aligned with the desired outcomes.

Furthermore, prompt engineering helps in improving efficiency and reducing the time and effort required to accomplish complex tasks. By leveraging the power of AI, prompt engineering allows us to automate processes, generate reports, and create comprehensive deliverables with speed and accuracy. This not only saves valuable time but also enhances productivity and enables us to focus on higher-value activities.

Moreover, prompt engineering enhances the interpretability and transparency of AI models. By structuring prompts that explicitly state the role, goal, and benefit, we create a clear framework for the AI model to follow. This facilitates better understanding and evaluation of the generated outputs, making it easier to validate the results and ensure they align with the intended objectives.

Prompt engineering is a fundamental component in harnessing the capabilities of AI models. By carefully structuring prompts using the Role - Goal - Benefit model and incorporating specific details, we can guide AI models to generate outputs that are tailored to our requirements. With its ability to streamline processes, improve efficiency, and enhance interpretability, prompt engineering is a valuable technique that empowers us to leverage the full potential of AI technology in various industries and applications.

CHAPTER 11: PRACTICAL EXAMPLES AND APPLICATIONS
EXERCISE

1. Write a summary of how the RGB model is used in a practical application of your choice.

2. Discuss potential future applications of the RGB model.

CHAPTER 12
CONCLUSION AND FINAL THOUGHTS

Prompt engineering is a powerful technique that plays a crucial role in designing effective AI models. Throughout this guide, we have explored the key concepts, best practices, and practical applications of prompt engineering. As we conclude our journey, let's recap the important aspects and highlight the benefits of prompt engineering in AI.

Prompt engineering involves crafting precise and robust prompts that serve as instructions to guide AI models in their decision-making process. By following the Role - Goal - Benefit

(RGB) model, we can provide clear guidance to the AI models and ensure that the generated outputs meet our specific requirements.

Using the RGB model, we begin by clearly defining the role, which identifies the persona or position from which the prompt is given. This helps the AI model understand the context and generate responses that align with the intended purpose. The goal statement outlines the specific objective or task that needs to be accomplished. By stating the goal with clarity, we guide the AI model towards generating outputs that are in line with the desired outcome. Finally, the benefit statement explains the advantages or value that can be derived from achieving the goal. This component helps the AI model understand the purpose and impact of the generated outputs.

By incorporating the RGB model into prompt engineering, we can generate outputs that are precise, relevant, and aligned with our objectives. The use of natural language and avoidance of ambiguous prompts further enhances the effectiveness of prompt engineering. By being concise and focused in prompt design, we provide the necessary guidance to AI models, allowing them to generate accurate and meaningful responses.

Contextual consideration is another important aspect of prompt engineering. By understanding the specific context in which the prompt will be used, we can design prompts that are tailored to the target audience or domain. Incorporating domain-specific knowledge and using active verbs adds energy and relevance to the prompts, resulting in more effective AI models.

One of the key advantages of prompt engineering is its ability to generate high-quality outputs that meet the needs and expectations of users. By crafting prompts with precision and providing specific details, we can ensure that AI models generate outputs that are in line with our requirements. This leads to improved efficiency, enhanced decision-making, and increased productivity in various industries and applications.

Challenges of Prompt Engineering

Prompt engineering is a critical aspect of working with large language models (LLMs) like GPT-3 or GPT-4, shaping their outputs and influencing the interaction between users and the AI. However, despite its significance, prompt engineering is still in its infancy and presents several challenges.

Novelty and Lack of Established Best Practices

One of the primary challenges in prompt engineering is its relative novelty. As a new discipline, there is a lack of comprehensive research, proven best practices, and standardized methodologies. This lack of well-established norms means that much of the prompt design currently depends on trial and error, intuition, and experimentation.

Due to the high degree of experimentation involved, consistency can be difficult to achieve. For instance, minor changes in the way a prompt is phrased can lead to substantial differences in the output from the model, which can sometimes be unexpected. This inherent unpredictability is a significant challenge in creating reliable and consistent systems based on these models.

Moreover, creating effective prompts can be complex. For the language model to understand and appropriately respond to the prompt, the engineer needs to consider numerous factors. These may include the clarity of the task or question, context provision, potential bias in the model's response, and more. Since there's no clear-cut formula or methodology to follow, it can be challenging to ascertain if a prompt is robust and well-constructed.

Evolution of Language Models

Another challenge stems from the constant evolution and updating of LLMs. With each iteration, these models are becoming more advanced and their responses more nuanced. As a result, the practices that worked well with earlier versions might not be as effective with newer ones.

The continual updates to the models mean that prompt engineers need to stay abreast of the latest developments and adapt their strategies accordingly. This requires constant learning and adjustment, adding to the complexity of the field.

Moreover, as the models evolve, so does their understanding and interpretation of prompts. This can lead to shifts in how a model responds to a given prompt over time, necessitating continuous testing, evaluation, and adjustment of prompts.

The Future of Prompt Engineering

Despite the challenges, the future of prompt engineering appears promising and full of potential. As the field matures, it's likely to transform how we interact with computers, and more broadly, AI systems.

One of the most exciting prospects is the shift towards more natural and intuitive human-computer interaction. With advanced prompt engineering, users could instruct computers using natural language, without needing to understand complex programming languages or coding paradigms. This would make powerful AI tools more accessible and usable to a broad range of people.

Further, as best practices for prompt engineering develop and become standardized, the process of generating useful prompts will likely become more efficient. This will lead to a wider adoption of LLMs across numerous fields, including education, healthcare, entertainment, and business.

Research into how different prompts influence an AI's responses will also continue to be an important part of developing more predictable and reliable AI systems. And as our understanding of these systems improves, so too will our ability to engineer prompts that elicit the desired outputs.

Lastly, the future of prompt engineering could see more personalized AI interactions. By tailoring prompts based on a user's specific needs, preferences, or context, AI systems could provide highly personalized responses and solutions, enhancing user experience and system effectiveness.

In conclusion, while prompt engineering is a relatively new discipline with inherent challenges, it holds enormous potential. With ongoing research and development, prompt engineering is likely to revolutionize our interaction with AI, making it more intuitive, reliable, and personalized.

As we conclude this guide, I encourage you to embrace the RGB model and follow prompt engineering best practices in your AI endeavors. By adopting these techniques, you can harness the power of prompt engineering to generate more accurate, relevant, and valuable outputs from AI models.

Furthermore, prompt engineering is a skill that can be further developed through training and coaching. If you are interested in expanding your knowledge and expertise in AI and prompt engineering, I invite you to explore further educational opportunities. Whether you want to enhance your AI artistry or master the intricacies of prompt engineering, additional training can empower you to unlock the full potential of AI technology.

In conclusion, prompt engineering is a critical aspect of designing effective AI models. By applying the RGB model and following prompt engineering best practices, we can generate precise, relevant, and high-quality outputs that drive success in various industries. The benefits of prompt engineering are vast, from improved productivity and decision-making to streamlined processes and enhanced efficiency. As you continue your AI journey, remember the power of prompt engineering and the transformative impact it can have on your AI projects.

CHAPTER 12: CONCLUSION AND FINAL THOUGHTS

1. Reflect on how your understanding of AI has changed after reading this book.

2. Discuss what you believe the future of AI holds and why.

Appendix: AI chronological timeline

Milestones in the development of artificial intelligence:

1. **Antiquity**: Greek myths of Hephaestus and Pygmalion incorporated the idea of intelligent automata. Mechanical statues built in Egypt and Greece were believed to be capable of wisdom and emotion.

2. **10th century BC**: Yan Shi presented King Mu of Zhou with mechanical men, which were capable of independent motion.

3. **384 BC - 322 BC**: Aristotle described the syllogism, a method of formal, mechanical thought and theory of knowledge in his work Organon.

4. **3rd century BC**: Ctesibius invents a mechanical water clock with an alarm. This was the first example of a feedback mechanism.

5. **1st century**: Hero of Alexandria created mechanical men and other automatons. He produced what may have been "the world's first practical programmable machine:" an automatic theatre.

6. **260 AD**: Porphyry wrote Isagogê which categorized knowledge and logic.

7. **800 AD**: Jabir ibn Hayyan developed the Arabic alchemical theory of Takwin, the artificial creation of life in the laboratory, up to and including human life.

8. **9th Century**: The Banū Mūsā brothers created a programmable music automaton described in their Book of Ingenious Devices: a steam-driven flute controlled by a program represented by pins on a revolving cylinder.

9. **1206**: Ismail al-Jazari created a programmable orchestra of mechanical human beings.

10. **1275**: Ramon Llull, Mallorcan theologian, invents the Ars Magna, a tool for combining concepts mechanically based on an Arabic astrological tool, the Zairja.

11. **~1500**: Paracelsus claimed to have created an artificial man out of magnetism, sperm, and alchemy.

12. **~1580**: Rabbi Judah Loew ben Bezalel of Prague is said to have invented the Golem, a clay man brought to life.

13. **Early 17th century**: René Descartes proposed that bodies of animals are nothing more than complex machines.

14. **1620**: Francis Bacon developed empirical theory of knowledge and introduced inductive logic in his work Novum Organum.

15. **1623**: Wilhelm Schickard drew a calculating clock on a letter to Kepler.

16. **1641**: Thomas Hobbes published Leviathan and presented a mechanical, combinatorial theory of cognition.

17. **1642**: Blaise Pascal invented the mechanical calculator, the first digital calculating machine.

18. **1672**: Gottfried Wilhelm Leibniz improved the earlier machines, making the Stepped Reckoner to do multiplication and division. He also invented the binary numeral system and envisioned a universal calculus of reasoning.

19. **1676**: Gottfried Wilhelm Leibniz derived the chain rule, which has become central for credit assignment in artificial neural networks.

20. **1726**: Jonathan Swift published Gulliver's Travels, which includes this description of the Engine, a machine on the island of Laputa, parodying Ars Magna.

21. **1750**: Julien Offray de La Mettrie published L'Homme Machine, which argued that human thought is strictly mechanical.

22. **1763**: Thomas Bayes's work An Essay towards solving a Problem in the Doctrine of Chances laid the foundations of Bayes' theorem.

23. **1769**: Wolfgang von Kempelen built and toured with his chess-playing automaton, The Turk, which was later shown to be a hoax, involving a human chess player.

25. **1800**: Joseph Marie Jacquard created a programmable loom, based on earlier inventions. Replaceable punched cards controlled sequences of operations in the process of manufacturing textiles.

26. **1805**: Adrien-Marie Legendre describes the least squares method, used widely in data fitting.

27. **1818**: Mary Shelley published the story of Frankenstein; or the Modern Prometheus, a fictional consideration of the ethics of creating sentient beings.

28. **1822–1859**: Charles Babbage & Ada Lovelace worked on programmable mechanical calculating machines, laying the groundwork for modern computing.

29. **1837**: The mathematician Bernard Bolzano made the first modern attempt to formalize semantics.

30. **1854**: George Boole investigated the fundamental laws of those operations of the mind by which reasoning is performed, thus inventing Boolean algebra.

31. **1863**: Samuel Butler suggested that Darwinian evolution also applies to machines, and speculates that they will one day become conscious and eventually supplant humanity.

32. **1943**: Warren McCulloch and Walter Pitts create a computational model for neural networks based on mathematics and algorithms called threshold logic.

33. **1950**: Alan Turing publishes "Computing Machinery and Intelligence", proposing what is now known as the Turing Test, a method for determining if a machine is intelligent.

34. **1956**: The Dartmouth Conference is held, where the term "Artificial Intelligence" is coined and the field is officially born.

35. **1957**: Frank Rosenblatt invents the Perceptron. The invention of the Perceptron marked the beginning of the field of neural network research.

36. **1964**: Daniel Bobrow's dissertation at MIT shows that computers can understand natural language to solve algebra word problems.

37. **1965**: Joseph Weizenbaum at MIT develops ELIZA, an interactive program that carries on a dialogue in English on any topic.

38. **1969**: The Stanford Research Institute develops Shakey, a robot that can move and react to its environment.

39. **1980**: The expert system, MYCIN, developed at Stanford University, could diagnose bacterial infections.

40. **1997**: IBM's Deep Blue beats world chess champion, Garry Kasparov, in a match.

41. **2006**: Geoff Hinton coins the term "deep learning" to explain new algorithms that let computers "see" and distinguish objects and text in images and videos.

42. **2011**: IBM's Watson wins Jeopardy against two former champions.

43. **2012**: Google's X Lab develops a machine that can independently browse the Internet and teach itself.

44. **2016**: Google's AlphaGo program beats a human professional Go player, the world champion, and several other top-ranked players in public matches.

45. **2021**: OpenAI releases GPT-3, a language model with 175 billion machine learning parameters. This model can generate human-like text based on a given prompt.

46. **2010**: Microsoft launched Kinect for Xbox 360, the first gaming device to track human body movement using just a 3D camera and infra-red detection.

47. **2011**: Mary Lou Maher and Doug Fisher organize the First AAAI Workshop on AI and Sustainability. In the same year, Apple's Siri, a smartphone app that uses natural language to answer questions, make recommendations and perform actions, is launched.

48. **2013**: Robot HRP-2 built by SCHAFT Inc of Japan, a subsidiary of Google, wins DARPA's Robotics Challenge Trials.

49. **2015**: Rupesh Kumar Srivastava, Klaus Greff, and Juergen Schmidhuber use LSTM principles to create the Highway network, a deep feedforward neural network. An open letter to ban development and use of autonomous weapons is signed by Hawking, Musk, Wozniak and 3,000 researchers in AI and robotics. Google DeepMind's AlphaGo defeats three-time European Go champion Fan Hui.

50. **2016**: Google DeepMind's AlphaGo defeats Korean Go champion Lee Sedol.

51. **2017**: The Asilomar Conference on Beneficial AI is held, discussing AI ethics and how to bring about beneficial AI while avoiding the existential risk from artificial general intelligence. Deepstack becomes the first published algorithm to beat human players in imperfect information games, as shown with statistical significance on heads-up no-limit poker. Google DeepMind's AlphaGo beats Ke Jie, the world No. 1 Go player at the time. Google DeepMind reveals that AlphaGo Zero—an improved version of AlphaGo—displayed significant performance gains while using far

fewer tensor processing units. AlphaZero masters chess in four hours, defeating the best chess engine, StockFish 8.

52. **2018**: Alibaba language processing AI outscores top humans at a Stanford University reading and comprehension test. Google announces Duplex, a service that allows an AI assistant to book appointments over the phone.

53. **2019**: DeepMind's AlphaStar reaches Grandmaster level at StarCraft II, outperforming 99.8 percent of human players.

54. **2020**: Microsoft introduces its Turing Natural Language Generation (T-NLG), the "largest language model ever published at 17 billion parameters". OpenAI's GPT-3, a state-of-the-art autoregressive language model is introduced.

55. **2022**: OpenAI debuts ChatGPT, an AI chatbot built on top of the GPT-3.5 large language model. It gains praise for its knowledge base and natural language responses, but also garners criticism for its tendency to "hallucinate," responding with factually incorrect answers with high confidence.

56. **2023**: By January, ChatGPT has more than 100 million users, making it the fastest growing consumer

application to date. OpenAI's GPT-4 model is released in March, a multimodal model allowing image input as well as text. Google releases its chatbot Google Bard, based on the LaMDA family of large language models, in response to ChatGPT.

57. **Present**: Artificial intelligence continues to evolve, advancing our understanding of learning, perception, problem-solving, and decision-making. AI technologies become integrated into everyday life, transforming industries, and raising new ethical and societal questions about their use and impact. AI's potential remains vast, and its future trajectory will likely continue to reshape our world in ways that are difficult to predict.

APPENDIX: AI CHRONOLOGICAL TIMELINE

1. Choose three events from the AI timeline and explain why you think they were significant in the development of AI.

2. Write a brief report on how one historical AI event of your choice has influenced modern AI techniques.

3. Predict what you think the next significant event or development might be in the field of AI, based on the historical timeline.

INDEX

About the Author

Phill C. Akinwale, PMP has managed operational endeavors, projects and project controls across government and private sectors in various companies, including Motorola, Honeywell, Emerson, Skillsoft, Citigroup, Iron Mountain, Brown and Caldwell, US Airways and CVS Caremark. With his extensive experience in various facets of Project Management and rigorous project controls, he has trained project management worldwide (NASA, FBI, USAF, USACE, US Army, Department of Transport) across five PMBOK® Guide editions over the last 15 years.

He holds twelve project management certifications with six in Agile Project Management (CSM, PMI-ACP, PSM, PSPO, PAL, SPS). As a John Maxwell Certified Coach and Speaker, Phill delivers workshops, seminars, keynote speaking, and coaching in leadership and soft skills. Working together with you and your team or organization, he will guide you in the desired direction and equip you to reach your goals. Books he has authored include: The No-Good Leader, Earned Value Basics and Project Management Mid-Level to C-Level.

www.ingramcontent.com/pod-product-compliance
Lightning Source LLC
LaVergne TN
LVHW022323060326
832902LV00020B/3642